DATE DUE

MAY 2 0 2001

PUERTO RICO

Island of Contrasts

by Geraldo Rivera
Pictures by William Negron

Parents' Magazine Press · New York

Library of Congress Cataloging in Publication Data

Rivera, Geraldo.
     Puerto Rico: island of contrasts.

     (Finding-out books)
     SUMMARY: Discusses the history, people, and
culture of this island commonwealth and the life-style
and problems of the Puerto Ricans who have migrated
to the mainland in search of jobs.
     1. Puerto Rico—Juvenile literature.
[1. Puerto Rico]   I. Negron, William, illus.
II. Title.
F1958.3.R56   917.295'03   72-14141
ISBN 0-8193-0683-5

Contents

Chapter One

Where Is Puerto Rico?

Puerto Rico is a crowded, sunny island of many different colors. It has green trees, fields and forests, brown hills, gray factories, and white, sandy beaches. And it all floats on the beautiful, blue waters of the Caribbean Sea.

If you draw a straight line on a map, Puerto Rico is about 1,700 miles from New York City and 1,100 miles from Miami, Florida.

It shares the Caribbean Sea with its large neighbors, Cuba, Jamaica, Haiti, and the Dominican Republic, and also with the Virgin Islands and almost 7,000 smaller islands. Together these islands are called the West Indies. They are called that because of a big mistake Christopher Columbus made a long time ago.

It was on his second trip to the New World in

1493. But Columbus still didn't know he had found the New World. He thought he had found a new way to get to India. That's why he called the Caribbean islands the Indies. Of course, Columbus was wrong in his geography. But since he was the brave and adventurous man who discovered the New World, and since he was right about so many other things, out of respect to him the islands are still called Indies, but now they are the West Indies.

Chapter Two
What is Puerto Rico?

Make believe that all the nations in the world belong to one big family. Maybe the United States could be a father, and the Soviet Union could be a mother. Great Britain could be an uncle, France an aunt. China could be a son, and perhaps Japan could be a daughter, and so on. In this family of nations, Puerto Rico would be only a step-child.

You see, Puerto Rico isn't really a country, but it's not really a part of the United States of America either. It's kind of half and half. People born in Puerto Rico are American citizens, but they aren't allowed to vote in our elections. They don't have to pay income taxes, but they do get drafted into the Army. They get a chance to elect their own governor, but Puerto Rico is not a state. In the United Nations, Puerto Rico is considered part of the United States, but the island is not really represented in the U.S. Congress. They have a congressman, but he isn't allowed to vote.

Are you confused? Maybe a short trip into the history of this half country, half state will clear things up.

Chapter Three
A Short Trip Back into History

Christopher Columbus discovered the lovely island of *Boriquén* on November 19, 1493. At the time he decided to call it *San Juan Bautista* (St. John the Baptist), in honor of Juan, the son of King Ferdinand and Queen Isabella of Spain. Columbus did that because the king and queen gave him the money to buy the ships he used to sail to the New World.

Now Boriquén wasn't exactly empty when Columbus found it. The tropical paradise was inhabited by the first Puerto Ricans. They were an Indian tribe called the *Taínos*. The Taínos were very gentle and peace-loving. The experts say that when Columbus first saw the island of Boriquén, about 30,000 Indians were living there. And they were doing pretty well. As a matter of fact, the Taínos were the ones who first discovered the uses of corn, rubber, and tobacco.

But the Spaniards didn't really appreciate the Taínos. They took advantage of them, and even made them slaves. This made the Indians very angry. Finally, when the cruel treatment was just too much to put up with, they revolted. That was in 1510. But the revolt didn't stand a chance. The

Spaniards had guns, and all the Taínos had were bows and arrows. When it was finally over in 1514, there were only 4,000 Indians left on the whole island. The name of Boriquén was changed to Puerto Rico (rich port), and little Puerto Rico became the property of big Spain. It has been the property of some bigger country ever since.

During the time that Puerto Rico was a colony of Spain, the people of the island could have been divided into three different groups: the rulers, the poor, and the African slaves brought in to work on the coffee and sugar-cane plantations.

The Spaniards were the rulers. They had all the good jobs in the Army, they owned all the best land and the biggest businesses. Even the priests in the Puerto Rican churches were from Spain.

Mostly, the poor people were the Indians, the mulattos (part Indian, part Spanish), the black slaves, and the small number of black people who had been given their freedom. Since the Spanish rulers had taken the few riches of the island, the poor got only the left-overs. They got the slums of the city of San Juan, and when they got land, it was the poorest land, far from the ports and high in the hills. And on that land, these *jíbaros* (peasants) could afford to build only small Indian-style huts. Despite its name, "rich port," Puerto Rico was not a very rich place, even in these early days. About the only valuable thing to be found there was a small amount of gold. The Spaniards used the Indians who were left to mine the gold for them.

But by the year 1600, all the gold was gone, and many Spaniards left the island. After this gold rush ended, the people who stayed in Puerto Rico found another way to earn a living. It was called piracy! By this time, the whole Caribbean Sea area, including Puerto Rico, had become a pirates' nest. They robbed the merchant ships and they raided the ports of the smaller islands. And for the next hundred years, many people in Puerto Rico were pirates who roamed the high seas to rob ships of their cargo.

Chapter Four

Time Goes By

As time went by, changes took place. People from all over the world started coming to Puerto Rico again. Its population grew as black people, red people, brown people, and white people moved there. Puerto Rico became a melting pot, where Indians and farmers and pirates and slaves and Spaniards and other people of different races and different continents intermarried and blended

together. Spain was still the mother country, but
Spain was far, far from the island of Puerto Rico. A
one-way trip on one of the great sailing ships of
that time took as long as three months. Separated
by almost 4,000 miles of ocean, Puerto Rico drifted
away from Spain.

For one thing, living so far away, the islanders

thought of themselves as Puerto Ricans and not as
Spaniards. Many of them, especially the poor
peasants, resented the Spanish land-holders and
shopkeepers. Many Puerto Ricans wanted Spain to
give them the freedom to choose their own
government. But Spain refused.

History books show that it takes a lot to make
Puerto Ricans angry. It took more than 350 years of
Spanish rule for them to get mad enough at Spain
to try a second revolution. It started in the small
town of Lares, on September 24, 1868. But like the
uprising of the Taíno Indians way back in 1510, this
revolt also failed.

After the failure of the Lares revolt, Puerto
Ricans again asked Spain for independence. But
Spain again refused. She refused until July 25, 1898,
405 years after Columbus discovered *la isla del
encanto* (the enchanted island). That was the day
the United States of America invaded the Spanish
colony of Puerto Rico. Spain and the United States
had declared war on each other!

Chapter Five

Puerto Rico Has a Change of Rulers

Most native Puerto Ricans were very happy. They thought that the United States had come to free their island from Spain. They thought that, finally, after 400 years of foreign rule, their island would become a free country. But they were wrong. Puerto Rico became a colony of the United States. It was still the property of a bigger country and it was still not free to make any of its own decisions.

And that was how Puerto Rico remained, until July 25, 1952. Exactly 54 years after the United States invaded Puerto Rico, the island was given a new form of government. Under the leadership of a great statesman named Luis Muñoz Marín, Puerto Rico was declared a commonwealth. It's still not a free country, and it's still not one of the states of the United States, but at least it's not just a colony any more.

Being a commonwealth means that the Puerto Rican government is allowed to take care of most of the things on the island, such as which roads to fix, or what buildings to build. But the United States government is still in charge of most of Puerto Rico's business with the rest of the world, such as which other countries Puerto Rico is allowed to be friends with, or which foreigners will be allowed to visit the step-child of the family of nations.

Chapter Six

Puerto Rico Today

Modern-day Puerto Rico is changing very fast. It used to be a place where almost everybody worked with the land, but now only a small percentage of Puerto Ricans are farmers. Where did all the farmers go? That's a very good question.

The most important crop in the economy of Puerto Rico used to be sugar cane. And many, many thousands of islanders made their living by growing the cane and then selling it to be refined into sugar or made into molasses or rum. But some bad things happened around 1930. They were so bad that they just about ended the sugar-cane days.

Hard Times

One of these things was the Great Depression. It was the same one that upset things here in the United States so much. When the stock market crashed, businesses went broke by the thousands. Millions of working people lost their jobs in the United States and in Puerto Rico. With no jobs, most had very little money. Things were bad in the United States, but they were much worse in Puerto Rico. The price of sugar, the main crop, fell way down. It went so low that the sugar-cane farmers could hardly make enough money to buy food for their own families to eat. To make matters even worse, it was getting harder and harder to grow sugar cane in Puerto Rico. After hundreds of years of growing nothing else, the land was worn out,

and the cane wouldn't grow very well. And last but not least, there were the *huracánes* (hurricanes). Two really bad storms destroyed the crops and made the farmers' life even tougher.

It got so tough that many decided that farming was not such a good idea any more.

During that period, hundreds of thousands of poor people began moving to the United States. They were searching for decent jobs and a better life, like the Irish, the Italians, and all the other immigrants who had come before them. But that was something many of them never found.

For many, many thousands who stayed in Puerto Rico, however, things were even worse. There was no work, and most people were very poor. The average Puerto Rican, during those hard times, earned only about $118 a *year!* That's only about $2.50 a week.

"Operation Bootstrap"

Life was like that on the island until the late 1940s and early 1950s. That's when things started to look up a little. The governments of the United

States and Puerto Rico got together and said, "we have to get things moving again." So they made a plan and called it "Operation Bootstrap." The idea was to get big companies from the United States to go to Puerto Rico and build factories.

Once the factories were built on the island, lots of people were hired to work in them. And because of that, many of those who used to be farmers are now factory workers. They still don't earn even half as much as working men and women in the United

States do, but at least now most Puerto Ricans have enough to buy food, clothing, and a place to live.

Rediscovery

And there was another thing that happened to make life a little easier for Puerto Ricans. Their island was discovered again, but not by Christopher Columbus. This time it was discovered by American tourists. You see, Puerto Rico has something that most of the mainland does not have—summer weather all year round.

The island is now visited by more than a million tourists every year. They come because of the sun and the sandy beaches and the golf courses. They spend money in Puerto Rico, and that means more jobs for the people there.

The summery weather makes it a really nice place to go, especially when it's winter up here; but if you go to Puerto Rico, don't expect to see a tropical paradise any more. A lot of the land, that used to be palm trees and beautiful scenery, is now covered by highways, hotels, factories, and big cities. You

have to travel far away from the capital, which is the city of San Juan, if you want to find the farms and hills that still have palm trees and tropical forests on them.

If you do get a chance to drive away from the city, it will be like driving at least 100 years back in time. In the middle of the island, far from the cities and their suburbs, you can still find the jíbaros living in their tiny shacks. Their rickety houses are made of wood, cardboard, and tin, and are built onto the sides of the steep hills. Many of the

shacks look as if they are going to tumble down the hill any minute. Most of the jíbaros are still very poor and for them not much has changed in the last 450 years.

And talking about old places, there's even one right in the city of San Juan. It's a section of the capital that is called *Viejo San Juan* (Old San Juan). In that part of the city, most of the buildings go back to the years when Spain ruled Puerto Rico. There are homes and old forts and Spanish-style plazas that are more than four hundred years old. The streets are old and very narrow. Walking down

one of them, you can imagine for a little while that you're living in the year 1700.

Today

So how can you describe modern-day Puerto Rico? Well, if you look very hard, it can still be a place of sleepy little towns with small, old houses, and town plazas dating back to the colonial times. And there are still some empty fields, and untouched hills and rivers and lonely beaches, but not as many as you might think. Puerto Rico has become very modern very quickly. This is especially true of the northern coast of the island, the side most often visited by tourists. As a matter of fact, that part of Puerto Rico is beginning to look more and more like the crowded parts of the mainland.

Chapter Seven

What Is a Puerto Rican?

Now don't laugh. That question isn't really as silly
as it sounds. Of course, Puerto Ricans are people
who live in, or come from the island of Puerto
Rico, but are they white or black or brown? Are
they short or tall? Are Puerto Ricans people with
straight hair or curly hair or hair that's fuzzy? The
answer is that Puerto Ricans are all these things.

They are a mixture of the different races and the different people who have come to the island from the beginning.

The first ingredient in the Puerto Rican recipe was the Taíno Indians we talked about in Chapter 3. Then into the mix went the Europeans, mostly from Spain, who settled and ruled the island for 400 years. Finally, added to this melting pot were the black people, the slaves who were brought in from Africa to work in the mines or on the sugar-cane plantations. The slaves were finally set free on March 22, 1873. That's about 10 years after they were freed on the mainland of the United States.

So, while some Puerto Ricans are all white, and others are all black, most are mixtures somewhere in between. Not all white. Not all black. But all Puerto Rican!

Chapter Eight

What Are the People of Puerto Rico Like?

Language

Because Spain ruled Puerto Rico for so long, Spanish was the only official language of the island. Today, almost all Puerto Rican people still speak Spanish, except some of those who were born and raised in the United States.

If you walk around the small villages or market places of Puerto Rico, Spanish is still the only language you will hear. But in San Juan, or in Ponce, or in the other big cities, there are many

Puerto Ricans who also speak English. About half of all Puerto Rican people understand some English; only about one out of every ten can speak it perfectly. But if you stay in one of the big hotels, almost everybody there speaks English.

Schools

When the United States first took over Puerto Rico in 1898, it made a rule that English was to be the only language spoken in the classrooms of the island. The idea behind this rule was to

"Americanize" the Puerto Rican people as soon as possible. This was not a very nice thing to do. Just imagine how you would feel if somebody came into your school and said that from now on only Spanish would be spoken in the classrooms of the United States.

Well, because it made a lot of people angry, the "English-only" rule was changed in 1948. Now both Spanish and English are spoken in the public schools of Puerto Rico.

Education used to be only for the rich children of the island. When Spain ruled Puerto Rico, only one out of every ten children was allowed to go to school. About 70 years ago, things finally started getting a little better. But it wasn't until the 1950s that every school-age boy and girl finally got the chance for an education.

What are the schools in Puerto Rico like? Like the schools here in the United States, some are good, others not so good, and some are really bad. The Puerto Rican schools in the worst shape are

those located far from the cities, in the countryside.
These public schools are often the kind of one-room
schoolhouses that you read about in stories of our
Wild West. The *campesino* (peasant) children who
go to these country schools are very poor. Many of
them have to walk to school with no shoes to wear.

The schools that are closer to Puerto Rico's big towns and cities are more like those in the United States. But there are still some differences. For example, in most grade schools in Puerto Rico the students wear special school uniforms. Boys wear dark pants and white shirts, and girls wear a certain color skirt and a white blouse. So it's easy to tell which school somebody goes to, just by looking at the color of his or her uniform.

Even the modern school buildings in Puerto Rico look different from school buildings in the United States. Because it's always summer in Puerto Rico, most of the schools have no glass windows. They have metal or wooden shutters that are left open, except when it rains or if a hurricane hits the island.

Education would be much better if more schools could be built. Many schools are overcrowded, and others are too old. The run-down schools that are

located in the terrible *arrabales* (slums) near San
Juan, and many of the country schools, have to be
replaced before all Puerto Rican children, rich or
poor, have the same chance for a good education.

What Do They Like to Eat?

The Puerto Rican style of cooking specializes in
tasty fried foods. Some of the favorites are *bistec*
(fried beefsteak) and *cuchifritos* (fried pork). Then
there's *arroz con pollo* (chicken with rice), and at
almost every meal, morning or night, there's rice
and beans. *Pasteles* are also big favorites. They're
meat, potatoes, and spices wrapped in a soft dough.
The whole thing is fried and it tastes great. And,
finally, there's *lechon asado,* the traditional roasted
pig that is served on many holidays and other
special occasions.

What About Holidays?

Puerto Rico and the United States share many of the same holidays. Among these are Christmas, Easter, and New Year's Day. But there are also many *días de fiestas* (holidays) that are celebrated only by the Puerto Rican people. One of these is *Día de los tres Reyes* (Three Kings Day). It falls on the 6th of January, and is celebrated just like another Christmas Day. People exchange gifts, and eat special holiday dinners together. That means the Puerto Rican people get *two* Christmases every year!

During the Christmas season, which lasts all the way from December 24 until January 6, the friendliness and the traditions of the people of the island really shine out in all their glory. It's a time when families come together from all over Puerto Rico. Many relatives living in the United States try their best to get "home" for the holidays.

Groups of people go from one neighbor's house to another. They sing Spanish songs together, and have a good time. This is a time of celebration, even for the poor people of the island. It is when they spend the little money they have saved to buy gifts for others, and also to get a big pig for roasting. And this is when they make the hot, homemade drinks, the kinds that make your head dizzy and your heart light.

There are other *días de fiestas* in Puerto Rico. There is one that marks the day Columbus discovered the island (November 19, 1493), one that marks the day Puerto Rico's constitution was signed (July 25, 1954), and many other big days.

There are also lots of little holidays. Almost every town on the island celebrates the birthday of the saint it has chosen as its favorite. These are not just one-day birthday parties; sometimes they go on for a whole week.

During this time, the town is decorated with many flowers, lovely floats, and everybody wears colorful costumes. Parades march around the town squares, and gay music fills the air. This is the time people show the pride they have in their home towns.

What Do Puerto Ricans Do For Fun?

The people of the island love sports. Their national game is borrowed from the United States. It's baseball! There are six professional teams in Puerto Rico, and when they play the fans go wild.

Many of the famous Puerto Rican baseball players, like Roberto Clemente of the Pittsburgh Pirates, play in both the American major leagues and in the Puerto Rican major leagues.

Basketball is the second most popular sport. Every high school and college has a team. The national team of Puerto Rico always does really well when playing against the teams of other countries in the Olympics and the Pan American games.

Horse racing, boxing, and professional wrestling are also very popular with the people of Puerto Rico. They love to bet on who is going to win.

In many small towns, and even in some basements and back rooms of the big cities, another kind of sport is played. It is called cockfighting. Two big roosters are made angry so they will fight each other. Inside a circle of people, the roosters face each other. Feathers fly as they attack, and bets are placed on which will be the winner. Sometimes the fight is to the death. Many Puerto Ricans feel that this sport is too cruel, and it has now been declared against the law.

Chapter Nine

How Many Puerto Ricans There Are, Where They Live, and How

There are about four and a half million Puerto Ricans in the world. About three million live on the island and most of the others live in the United States.

Some Puerto Ricans are very rich and live on

their island in big, beautiful homes near the ocean. Many of the traditions and customs of their lives are borrowed from the years of Spanish rule. Once in a while they get dressed up in the old-style costumes to remind the world of their Spanish heritage. The women wear the lace and flowing dresses of colonial times, and the gentlemen wear the traditional suits of the old Spanish nobility.

Many other wealthy Puerto Rican people have a style of life that is more like that of the United States. They live in the hundreds of shiny, new apartment buildings that have been built in the city of San Juan in recent years. Their lives are a lot like those of successful American businessmen and their families who live in the big buildings of Manhattan, Chicago, or San Francisco. They dress like the people in those cities, too.

The children of the rich families of Puerto Rico usually go to private schools. And even these schools have become "Americanized." Almost all the classes in the private schools are still taught in English.

Sometimes many generations of the same family live together in one big house. In the city of Bayamon, near San Juan, there is what could be called a typical Puerto Rican family. It is the home of Juan and Tomasa Rivera. Papa Juan, the *abuelo* (grandfather), is 95 years old. Mama Tomasa, the *abuela* (grandmother), is 92 years old. Three of their sons also live in the same house. Augustine, Claudio, and Ramon are grown men with families of their own. But because the old house is big enough, and because families in Puerto Rico stay closer than most families in America, grandparents, parents, and children all live together.

The Rivera family shows how much Puerto Rico has changed in the last three generations. Papa Juan and Mama Tomasa remember the days when Spain was the ruler of Puerto Rico. For many years, they

lived in the countryside, near the big sugar-cane
plantations. Papa Juan was a supervisor in the fields.
He rode around on a big horse and talked with the
cane workers. Because Papa Juan was a kind and
considerate person, the workers called him "Don"
Juan. Don is the title Puerto Rican people give
somebody they respect.

But time passed, and many of the sugar-cane plantations closed during the Depression. Papa Juan and Mama Tomasa had to move to the city. They didn't like it as much as their home in the country, but it was closer to the factories and to the offices where Augustine, Claudio, and Ramon found jobs. Two of their other children, Cruz and Anna, came to the United States in 1940. Because they found the new life they were looking for, both of them still live in the United States but would like to go back to Puerto Rico some day.

So now Papa Juan and Mama Tomasa live in their house with three of their sons, three daughters-in-laws, and about ten grandchildren. Abuelo and Abuela remember "old" Puerto Rico. Some of their grandchildren live in "new" Puerto Rico. Some of them attend the University of Puerto Rico. They wear the latest style American clothes, and two of them even drive their own cars.

But while they are at home, they all follow the rules of "old" Puerto Rico.

The table in the dining room isn't big enough for everybody to sit down all at once, so the men eat first. Papa Juan sits at the head of the table, his sons sit closest to him, and his grandsons sit at the other end of the table. Even though she is 92 years old, Mama Tomasa supervises the serving of the meal. When all the food is on the table, Papa Juan says a prayer, and then the men eat. Later, after they have finished, the women and small children eat.

You see, the women of "old" Puerto Rico still haven't been liberated.

In recent years, the working people of the island have also begun to live like other working people in the United States. The Puerto Rican man or woman who works in a bank, or factory, or office building, lives in a small, neat house located in the *urbanizaciones* (suburbs). Of course, the houses look a bit different from those in American suburbs. In

the Puerto Rican *urbanizacion,* the newer houses
are made of cement, because it stays cooler in the
hot weather, and lasts longer. Like the school
buildings, these houses have no need for windows,
nor any other protection against the cold of winter.

It is only in *el campo* (the countryside) that the

old way of Puerto Rican life has not been changed. In el campo, the families still grow their own food on their tiny pieces of land. And it is only in el campo that you can find barefoot boys and girls helping their parents bring the crops down from the hills to the marketplace of *el pueblo* (the town). And

on market day, in the old town plazas, you can still watch as farmers trade their crops for shoes, clothing, and other things that they can't make for themselves.

But el campo is a style of life that is fast disappearing. More and more farms are being made into hotels, housing developments, and factories. And, as we said, life in Puerto Rico is becoming more and more like life here in the United States.

Chapter Ten

Puerto Ricans on the Mainland

Where the Good News Ends

Even though great steps forward have been made, hundreds of thousands of Puerto Ricans are still very poor. There is not enough work for everybody, and almost three out of every ten people do not have jobs. No job means no money, and no money means that many have to live in slums or country shacks, and wear old, worn-out clothes. That's sad.

Because it was so hard to find a job on the island of Puerto Rico, many, many people over the last 30 years left to find a new life on the mainland. Most of them—more than a million and a half—came to live in the cities of New York, Illinois, New Jersey, and Pennsylvania.

But the sad story doesn't end with this trip to the United States.

Where Did They Go?

The search for jobs and a better life led the Puerto Ricans to the great cities of America. They came by the thousands to New York City, Philadelphia, Chicago, and Newark. Some found good jobs and could afford to live decently. But most could not speak English and had no job training. They got the leftover jobs, for the lowest pay. Jobs like dishwashers in hotels and janitors for rundown tenements.

They were poor when they got here, and most are still poor.

Where Do They Live?

Like most poor people, the Puerto Ricans in New York and the other cities got the worst houses to live in. The slum buildings are very old, and many of them are filled with rats and cockroaches. The neighborhoods are filled with garbage and crime.

Even many of the schools in these areas are old, dirty, and crowded. To make matters worse, many of the Puerto Rican children going to those schools can't speak English. In the years it takes for them to learn English, they fall way behind in their studies. If the schools would teach classes in both English and Spanish, as they do in Puerto Rico, it would be a lot better.

It's Not All Bad News

Although most Puerto Rican people living here are still poor, things are slowly getting better. More and more are able to leave the slums of the big cities and move to nicer places. But it's taking such a long time.

Many Puerto Ricans, especially those who used to live on farms on the island, have a hard time getting used to life in places like New York or Chicago. In Puerto Rico, they lived in warm, quiet places, with trees and animals all around. But in the city, they are surrounded by big buildings, and lots of trucks and cars, and crowds of people. For many

Puerto Rican people, the change is too much to take. In recent years, more Puerto Ricans have been leaving the United States than are coming here.

How Are Puerto Ricans in the United States Different from Those in Puerto Rico?

Well, for one thing, they are getting more and more "Americanized." Especially those born in the United States. Many young men and women wear the newest style clothes, dance to rock-and-roll music, and speak English. Some have even forgotten

how to speak Spanish. But for the most part, the
Puerto Rican-American has two languages and two
cultures.

And, in fact, the Puerto Rican people have
changed the cities more than the cities have
changed the Puerto Rican people. Just walk around
New York City some day. You'll be surprised to see
the hundreds of advertising signs that are written in
Spanish. Spanish music is getting very popular, and
there are two Spanish-language TV stations.

What Now?

I wish I knew for sure. I wish I could say that the future was rosy for the Puerto Rican people, but nobody really knows. Nobody even knows if Puerto Rico will remain a commonwealth of the United States. Many people want a change. Some say that Puerto Rico should become the 51st State of the United States. Others say that Puerto Rico should become a free country. But whatever happens, many Puerto Ricans will be poor for a long, long time. And that includes those living on the island of Puerto Rico and those living here in the United States. As I said, things seem to be getting a little better, but it is taking such a long time. Maybe, with a little luck, lots of hard work, and some help from our friends, Puerto Rico and Puerto Ricans will make it. We hope so.

Pronunciation Guide

Puerto Rico	PWER-toh RI-koh
Boriquén	Boh-RIN-ken
San Juan Bautista	San-wahn Boh-TEES-ta
Taínos	Taa-EE-nose
jíbaros	HE-bah-rose
El Grito de Lares	El GRI-toh day LA-res
la isla del encanto	lah ESS-la dell en-KAN-toh
Luis Muñoz Marín	LOU-ees MOON-yohs mah-RINE
huracánes	U-ra-KAN-es
Viejo San Juan	Vee-EH-ho San-wahn
Ponce	PON-say
campesino	kam-peh-SEE-no
arrabales	ah-rah-BAL-es
Bayamon	buy-a-MONE
abuelo	ah-BWEL-oh
abuela	ah-BWEL-ah
bistec	BEES-tik
cuchifritos	koo-chee-FREE-toes
arroz con pollo	ah-ROOS cone POY-yo
pasteles	pahs-TELL-es
lechon asado	leh-CHONE ah-SAH-doe
Días de fiestas	DEE-ahs day Fee-ES-tahs
Días los tres Reyes	DEE-ahs day los tress RAY-es
urbanizaciones	err-baan-nee-sah-SEE-oh-ness
el campo	el CAM-po
el pueblo	el PWE-blow

Index